Conte

Games

We Play

Some of the games we play today
were played by children long ago.
This picture is hundreds of years old.
It shows many of the games
that were played back then.
Some of these games are still
around today.

Can you
find these games
in the picture?

2

3

What's Old, What's New?

Take a look at the toys
children play with today.
Some of them were invented
a long time ago.
Other toys have
only just been invented.
Can you guess which toys are old
and which toys are new?

Old Wheels, New Wheels

Wheels have been around for thousands of years. They were invented to help people get from place to place. People soon learned that toys with wheels were lots of fun, too. Today those toys are fun *and* fast!

Skateboard Safety

Check that your skateboard is safe before you ride it.

Learn the easy moves before you try the hard moves.

Learn how to fall off your skateboard safely.

Always skateboard at a skateboard park – never on the road.

Always wear a helmet and elbow, knee, and wrist guards.

At the Skateboard Park

The Skateboard Champ

Whizzing, whooshing, wheeling,
racing down the ramp.
Whizzing, whooshing, wheeling,
I'm the skateboard champ.

With my feet on the deck
and the wind whistling past,
I hit the top of the ramp,
then zoom down really fast.

7

Many places have skateboard parks. Some parks run contests where skateboarders can show off their skills and tricks.

So sharpen your skills and try out your tricks. Maybe one day *you'll* be a skateboard champ!

Air The space under your board when you jump.

Bail To jump off your skateboard before you fall.

Flip Trick To flip the board when you're in the air.

Grind To slide your skateboard along an edge.

Road Rash What you get when you fall off your skateboard.

Board Talk

I jump and do a flip trick,
Then go grinding down a rail.
When, suddenly, my board spins out.
I think I'd better bail!

Frances Bacon

THE BUMP

Written by Diana Noonan   Illustrated by Lorenzo Van Der Lingen

The children liked the bump in the path.
They rode their bikes over it.
The bump was their favourite place to play.

14

The gardener didn't like
the bump in the path.

"It's too dangerous to have a bump
in the path," she said. "It will have to go!"

15

So the gardener got to work.
She jumped up and down
on the bump.

JUMP
JUMP
JUMP

THUMP
THUMP
THUMP

Then she hit the bump
with a spade, but it
still didn't budge.

16

Then the gardener rolled the bump
with a roller. It still didn't budge.
The bump wouldn't go away.
Everyone watched and smiled.

17

"That's a very tough bump,"
said the gardener,
wiping her face.
"I'll give a rammer a try."

BANG
BANG
STOMP
STOMP

It was no good.
The bump stayed a bump,
and the children
watched and smiled.

"There's only one thing to do,"
said the gardener.
"I'll have to give a bulldozer a try!"

It was no good.
The bump still stayed a bump,
and the children still watched and smiled!

19

"I know what
we can do," said Simon,
and he whispered
in the gardener's ear.

"That's a very good idea,"
said the gardener.

So the gardener built
a new path around
the bump and everyone was happy.

"Lucky us!" shouted the children.
"Now we have a new path
and we have a bump, too."

21

Riding

Written by Jill Meadowcraft

Photographed by Brian Enting

Wednesday is my favourite day at school. On Wednesdays, we go riding.

Hello!

When I arrive at the riding school, I say hello to my instructor. Then we go to see the ponies.

We all help groom the ponies.
I brush Pablo.
Pablo likes being brushed.
Pablo is my
favourite pony.

Next we put my
special saddle on Pablo.
It is made of sheepskin.
It is soft so I can feel
how the pony moves.
A sheepskin saddle makes
my muscles work hard, too.

My instructor helps
put on my helmet.
Her name is Bronwyn.

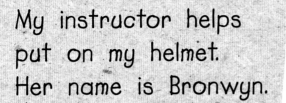

Bronwyn helps me
up on my pony.

Then she leads
Pablo and me
around the ring.

I do my exercises.
Bronwyn says
I am getting
good at them.

The exercise I like best
is leaning forward
to touch Pablo's mane with my face.
This exercise makes
my back muscles stronger.

Today, we have a race
on our ponies
to see who can carry
the most water
from one bucket
to another.

It is fun, but hard to do.
You have to be careful your pony
doesn't kick over the bucket.

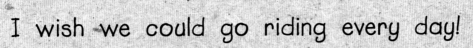

I wish we could go riding every day!

31

The Throw-Away Box

Written by Susan Stone   Illustrated by Marjorie Scott

It's too wet to play outside.

It was raining.
Ben and Kate were bored.
They didn't like being
stuck inside the house.
So Dad brought out
the throw-away box.

32

Just then, the doorbell rang.
In came their friends,
Sara and Ted.
The children looked
at the things
in the throw-away box.

We're looking
for ideas in
the throw-away box.

What
are you
doing?

Ben drew a face on
a big, brown paper bag.
He made two holes
so he could see.

34

Ben roared and chased Ted around the room. The children laughed and laughed.

Kate made a funny moustache.
Next she put on a black cape,
a black hat, and the funny moustache.
Then she found a ribbon.

The lion roared, but it got up on the chair. Then it stood up and roared and waved its paws.

The children looked at the things
in the throw-away box.
They made masks.
They made costumes.

The next day,
it was still raining.

But lots of friends came to the circus.
They clapped for the lion and the
ringmaster with the funny moustache.
They cheered on the juggler.
They laughed at the clown.

After the circus,
everyone had drinks and popcorn.

Then the children looked
at the things in the throw-away box.
"We could..." said Sara.

"Not now!" said Dad. "The rain has stopped.
Why don't you all go outside and play?"

SPORTS ARE FUN

Written by Pippa Cross

You can play sport in a team, or on your own. In team sports, everyone works together to play the game.

Rugby is a team sport played with an oval ball. Players can kick and throw the ball.

46

Many sports use balls.
These can be
thrown, kicked,
or hit with a bat.

Soccer
is played with
a round ball.
Players kick the ball,
or use their head
or body to hit it.

47

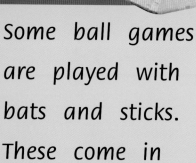

Some ball games are played with bats and sticks. These come in many shapes and sizes.

Ice hockey players use an L-shaped stick to hit a hard rubber disk called a puck. The players wear skates with curved steel blades.

Baseball bats are made of materials such as wood, metal, or plastic.

Games that use bats and sticks can be dangerous. Players often wear safety gear such as face masks, helmets, gloves, chest protectors, and leg guards.

49

In some sports, players throw a ball through a hoop and net. The aim of these games is to score more points than the other team.

Netball is a fast game. Players pass the ball to their end of the court, then shoot it through the net to score a goal.

Tennis is played on an outdoor or indoor court. A net goes across the middle of the court. There can be two or four players.

In some sports, players use bats or rackets to hit a ball over a net and back again. In other sports, such as volleyball, players hit a ball over a net with their hands.

51

Letters That Go Together

sp speeding, spins

wh wheeling, whizzing, whooshing

Sounds I Know

-ee speeding   **-zz** whizzing

-oo whooshing

Words That Go Together

doorbell   skateboard

ringmaster   spaceman

Words I Know

everyone	have	made	still
favourite	helps	next	then
friends	laughed	play	they
funny	let's	smiled	watched

52